EVERYTHING

I

KNOW ABOUT

TRUE LOVE

A Guide to Finding Happiness and True Love

Marilyn C. Patterson

CONTENT

CHAPTER ONE

What Love Is and Is Not in True Love

True love has been a subject of discussion for millennia. While cynics frequently deny its existence, hopeless romantics believe that everyone should search for their soul mate.

We have chosen to examine the psychological factors that cause love to blossom or fade in light of the recent scientific evidence that real love is not only attainable but also capable of lasting a lifetime.

Let's begin by stating what true love is in its purest form:

True Love: What Is It?

True love is a powerful and enduring affection shared by spouses or lovers who are in a meaningful, passionate, and joyful relationship. A couple that has been married for 45 years and is still devoted to and enthusiastic about the other is an example of real love.

The greatest way to conceptualize love is as a verb. Love is dynamic and has to be put into practice to flourish. As Dr. Paul observed, "We frequently spend our time thinking about how our spouse feels about us or how the relationship seems to others.

Even while it feels lovely to be loved by someone, each of us can only truly experience our loving sentiments for that person, not their feelings for us. We need to act lovingly if we want to connect with and maintain those love sentiments within ourselves. Otherwise, we may be inside a fiction.

Accepting the notion that the only person we truly control in a relationship is ourselves might at times feel irritating, but it's also rather liberating. Our portion of the dynamic is under our control. Therefore, we have a choice between acting in ways that undermine intimacy and acting in ways that are indicative of our love, compassion, affection, respect, and kindness. To make the latter decision deliberately and consistently, it is helpful to consider the qualities that Dr. Paul discovered to be essential to preserving a loving relationship throughout his more than 25 years of observing couples.

The "Couples Interactions Chart," which the father and daughter study team designed, contrasts the qualities of a perfect relationship to those of what Dr. Paul called a "fantasy bond," which shows the differences between the two.

The fantasy bond is an "illusion of closeness and connection [that] allows couples to maintain their love and loving fantasies while maintaining emotional distance." When partners choose the appearance of being in a relationship above genuine affection and intimacy, a fantasy connection develops. The sense of liveliness and attractiveness between people is lessened by this link.

True Love's Attributes vs. a Fantasy Bond

1. The ability to receive criticism without getting defensive or furious
Couples should be open with each other and willing to hear each other's comments without being defensive or negative to sustain their connection. Couples should seek out the glimmer of truth in their partner's statements, suggests Dr. Paul.

That fact can provide a critical hint as to how we can unknowingly be driving our spouse away. Listening to our partners naturally helps them feel seen, heard, and cared for, even if we don't always agree with what they have to say. Punishing our spouse for being open and upfront with us, on the other hand, stifles communication.

2. Availability to try new things vs resistance to them

When both parties are in touch with a vibrant, open, and vulnerable aspect of themselves that embraces novel experiences, a relationship will flourish. Even while we don't have to share all of our partner's interests, doing new things together, traveling, and breaking patterns may often provide our relationships with a fresh start and a feeling of renewal.

3. Integrity and honesty vs fraud and deceit

One of the earliest things that most of us learn as children are to always speak the truth. Nevertheless, in our closest relationships as adults, there may be a lot of dishonesty. We harm our spouse, the relationship, and ourselves greatly when we lie to our partner. Being honest with our spouses is the only way to build trust, which is necessary to feel vulnerable with them.

4. Respecting others' limitations, priorities, and objectives rather than going over them

We need to keep in mind that the other person is distinct from us to prevent a fantasy relationship. Respecting someone as a distinct, independent person entails doing just that. Many times, spouses adopt roles or participate in power dynamics.

We could instruct one another on what to do or how to act. Alternatively, we may use defining or constricting language to talk to and about one another. In essence, we don't consider them as distinct people but as extensions of ourselves. We therefore really reduce our attraction to them. We treat the other person as our right arm, according to Dr. Lisa Paul. When that happens, we are just as drawn to them as we are to our right arm.

5. Personal sexuality and physical affection against sexuality that is insufficient,

impersonal, or monotonous and lacks attachment

A big part of how we communicate love is via affection. Relationships can become stale when we shut ourselves off from our sentiments of love. As a result, there is less passion between us and our spouses. Both partners may feel more distant and unsatisfied when sexual activity is regular or impersonal. To keep love alive, we must stay connected to the part of ourselves that craves physical affection and is open to receiving it.

6. Recognition versus misinterpretation

It's simple to project onto our spouse or to misinterpret what they say, using them to feel attacked or harmed in ways that are emotionally resonant with us. It's also simple to become mired in our viewpoint without considering other people's viewpoints. We will never agree since we are two distinct individuals with independent thoughts.

However, it's crucial to make a sincere effort to comprehend our companion from a distinct point of view. Our spouse is much more likely to soften and see our side as well when they feel seen and understood.

7. Nonthreatening, non-threatening, and noncontrolling actions vs submission and dominance-based manipulations

The dynamics when one partner behaves like a parent and the other as a kid are common in relationships.

The other is looked to for advice, but when they are told what to do, they get resentful of them. Alternately, someone may try to exert control over the circumstance and then criticize the other person for being careless, immature, or compliant.

True love requires equality for a partnership to exist. Neither party is enjoying an adult, equal, and loving relationship when one person tries to dominate or manipulate the other, whether it is by yelling and screaming or by stonewalling and acting like the victim.

How to Build a True Love Relationship

How can we make changes in ourselves to foster a more loving relationship now that we are aware of the qualities of true love? Despite these apparent differences between true love and fantasy, it's crucial to note that many individuals still confuse the two. They could even choose fiction over reality since it hurts less to look attached to someone than it does to truly feel close to them.

A lot of us get sucked by fairy tales, superficial details, or interpersonal structures (i.e. how it looks as opposed to how it feels). Although the circumstance may make us feel connected or secure, we don't let ourselves get too close to the other person and instead fall in love with the illusion.

Because even though most of us claim to seek love, we frequently act in ways that drive it away. Consequently, knowing and confronting our barriers is the first step to being more loving.

1. Overcoming barriers that prevent true love from flourishing

Unbeknownst to them, many people have intimate relationship concerns. Even while we may be tolerant of our romantic fantasies coming true in our imaginations, we frequently find it intolerable when those fantasies become reality. According to Dr. Paul, being loved by someone puts our defenses in jeopardy and causes us to relive emotional trauma and childhood fear.

The way we think about ourselves negatively yet habitually is said to be disrupted by both giving and receiving love, according to this theory. "Unconsciously, we might feel that if we didn't push love away, the entire world as we have known it would shatter and we wouldn't know who we are."

Because of these factors, we are frequently the largest barrier to establishing and sustaining a love relationship. We must become aware of the barriers we present to love. For instance, if we experienced rejection as a child, we would worry about becoming too close to another individual. Because we may not feel that we can truly rely on or trust a partner, we may either cling to or fend off that person, both of which have the same effect of causing distance.

If we experienced criticism or resentment as children, we may struggle to feel confident or deserving in our relationships. Due to the danger to our early self-perception, we may seek out partners who treat us poorly in ways that feel familiar or we may never truly embrace our partners' emotions of the love for us.

We may completely shun relationships and feel pseudo-independent, or we may unconsciously seek out individuals who rely on us to supply all of their wants and more if we were intruded upon as children or if we had an "emotionally hungry" father. Again, both of these extremes might result in connections that aren't truly intimate and close.

The good news is that by learning more about ourselves and our defenses, we may begin to break these harmful relationship patterns. We pick the partners we do for a reason, right? What characteristics—both positive and negative—draw us in? Are there any tactics we may use to manipulate or entice our spouse into acting in a manner that supports our defenses? How do we put a barrier between us? What actions do we do that appear to be self-protective but instead turn the love away?

find out more about the aversion to closeness

2. Distinguishing yourself from the influences from the past that don't help you now

The technique of confronting ingrained, long-standing patterns and defenses—which Dr. Paul refers to as differentiation—has been further explored by him. These four steps make up the process:

We may live in a less protected condition and pursue our true desires in life by taking these steps toward distinction.

study differentiation more thoroughly

How to Maintain a Long-Lasting Love

By comprehending how and why we create a fantasy attachment, we may find several solutions to the question of why love eventually fades.

The strongest barrier against love is the imaginary relationship.

Even after we have let down our guard and allowed ourselves to fall in love, we may turn to a fantasy bond to help us maintain the illusion that we are not alone while maintaining emotional distance from our partner whenever we feel scared, whether it be of losing our partner or differentiating from our old, familiar identity.

In addition to avoiding the traits mentioned above, we should also take the following steps to prevent a fantasy attachment.

How to become more loving and dissolve a fantasy bond:

True love: what is it?

Be empathetic. Find every opportunity to connect, to express love and attraction.

Be mindful and take it slowly. Spend some time talking and listening to your spouse in depth.

Establish eye contact. Although it seems easy, we frequently forget to just glance at our companion.

Try a vintage item. Make time for your favorite hobbies to do together and keep them up.

Try a novel approach. Don't just settle into a routine. Continue offering new things to do and be receptive to suggestions from your spouse.

Break the mold. Be willing to interrupt the habit and create room for spontaneity if repeating the same thing over and over again makes you feel less excited.

Avoid being passive and in charge. Make an effort to have an equitable exchange of opinions. Don't try to dominate your spouse; instead, accept responsibility for your behavior.

Use "I" instead of "we" while speaking. Keep in mind that you will always be two distinct persons and try not to cross any lines that might make you less attractive.

Be conscious of your inner critic. Each of us has an inner adversary that judges ourselves, our partners, and our closest relationships.

Make an independent decision. You don't have to do everything as a pair just because you are one. Don't expect your spouse to give up the friendships and activities they like on their own, and don't give up anything you enjoy doing on your own either.

Express your emotions. Don't anticipate your spouse being able to read your thinking. You may prevent passive-aggressive or harsh methods of connecting by being clear when expressing what you want and feel. Inspires your spouse to follow suit as well.

A "tit for tat" mindset should be avoided. Each of us must decide to behave in love. Instead of being in touch with how nice it feels to be loving toward someone else, we start to set expectations and foster resentment when we start quantifying what we do for each other.

Encourage your partner to pursue their passions. Even if those things aren't what is most important to you, never stop empowering and supporting your spouse to be the most alive and to do the things that make them feel the most like themselves.

Make choices that your lover would deem loving. Make sure the things you do are things that are important to your partner personally. Even if you may enjoy receiving flowers, would your partner feel the same way about you?

Avoid closing yourself off. It's far too simple to shut down anytime we experience shame, worry, disappointment, or annoyance from our spouse, but we must struggle to avoid being closed off and turning away the love that is directed at us.

CHAPTER TWO

A Guide to Finding Happiness and True Love

Do you repeatedly find yourself in dating scenarios and wonder why your efforts to find love are failing? If you're unhappy and want to discover true, lasting love yet feel trapped. but have been constantly single for the majority of the previous three years. At that point, a reset is probably necessary.

It's time to reassess your dating life and consider what has been preventing you from finding the right partner. You are at the appropriate place if you don't know where to begin.

You may find it difficult to complete certain tasks while being able to complete others. Although this is typical, you must do something new if you want a different outcome.

whether you're ready to let go of whatever it is that could be stopping you. Your life will start to change at that point, and you'll be on a clearer and quicker route to finding the love you seek.

1. Refrain from accepting the wrong person
Finding the appropriate partner and rejecting the wrong one are both important aspects of dating. Sometimes you want a relationship and to be liked so badly that you stick with the first person who asks you

out regardless of whether you click with them or not.

It's crucial to be clear and assess what's going on with you if you keep dating or pursuing the wrong people. Determine what you truly want in life and relationships by taking the time to look inside. Knowing your basic values will help you determine whether a possible spouse is suited for you.

2. Stop Complaining That There Aren't Any Good Men In Your City From East to West, no matter who I speak with, everyone complains that their city is the worst for meeting men, but that isn't the case. All you need to do is look; great men are EVERYWHERE. They may be found

standing in line at Whole Foods, Starbucks, gyms, and beaches, among other places.

Instead of checking your phone every five minutes the next time you're out, keep your head up, keep your eyes open, and pay attention to your surroundings. I'm sure you'll be shocked by what you discover once you start searching regularly.

3. Stop comparing your life to others' lives. Your life is equally as valid as everyone else's, regardless of your circumstances, including your job, residence, friends, finances, and relationship status. Being single is okay; being in a relationship doesn't determine who you are. You establish who you are.

Have you heard the saying, "Comparison is the thief of joy?" Make gratitude your mentality. What would occur if you stopped evaluating yourself in comparison to others and instead showed gratitude for what you now have?

4. Give up the Attachment to the Result

Although dating should be enjoyable, many people find the experience to be intimidating and sad when they place too much emphasis on the success of their first or even third date. In the era of internet dating, this is especially true. You can find yourself on a never-ending cycle of dates if you don't control your expectations.

In most cases, it goes like this... You get ready and go meet him, wondering with anticipation, is it him? Has he found the right person for you? We have so many things in common that make us the ideal match. All of this is done before you even place a drink order.

You're already considering marriage and having children even though you don't even know this individual. Then, when things don't work out for whatever reason, you find yourself home exhausted and depleted emotionally.

Although everyone has ups and downs, the major distinction between happy individuals is how they see their setbacks and victories.

Have the mindset that you're going on a date to meet new people and have a nice time. Be observant. Being present Be attentive. Even if they aren't the proper person for you, you still had a blast or learned something new about what you value in a companion.

Every individual you meet is a step in the right way, so keep in mind that the early phases of dating aren't personal.

"When we display our vulnerability, the beautiful things in life come to us."

5. Stop surrounding your heart with barriers.
This entails being willing to be open-hearted and vulnerable. We've all experienced being harmed a few times, so building barriers may seem normal. But when we display our

vulnerability, the good things in life come to us.

This is a brand-new individual. No, not the one who injured you. Therefore, treating them as though they have or would in the future be unfair as you enter what may be a new relationship.

It's okay to feel uneasy, to have doubts, to be vulnerable, and to connect with your truest self.

6. Quit Counting on Others To Make You Happy
Do you live a life that is only a series of actions?

If you're like many of the individuals I deal with, your life has started to revolve around work, the gym, television, or the internet, and sleep with little to no enjoyment in between. If you ever meet "The One," you will be content, even though you aren't right now.

This thought is not only unreal but also stressful.

What emotions would you experience if someone unexpectedly showed up and demanded that you be their only source of joy? Your life should already be good, and a fantastic spouse shouldn't try to make it better.

Nobody can make you as happy as you can; happiness is something you create for yourself.

The journey to having the life you desire and feeling content begins with you, and it begins now, not later. Not sure what brings you joy? Learn more!

What piques your attention or keeps you wondering or thinking? Take action on the ideas that keep coming to mind repeatedly by beginning to investigate and pay attention to them.

It may resemble enrolling in an art class, picking up a new language, or returning to school. It can involve moving to a new place, going on a fantasy trip, or learning an instrument.

Whatever it is, just start moving in the direction of something that will bring you happiness and a sense of fulfillment.

7. Stop doubting yourself and start believing in yourself.

The most significant factor is this. Do you live as optimally as you can? Are your instincts and emotions being heard? Let go of your expectations or what other people have told you to do.
Regardless of what other people may say, follow your instincts and pay attention to your intuition.

8. Confide in yourself.

Although you'll be tested often on your ability to believe in yourself, it gets easier the more you do it. Believing in yourself requires practice. Your chances of finding a supportive mate increase as you grow in self-confidence.

How can you expect someone to believe in you if you don't?

It's an inside job, but you can find happiness and love.

Any of us find it difficult to change. We desire ease of use. To be sure, please. We desire a magic wand.

Although there are no magic wands, you may choose your path in life and lead the life you choose. If YOU were to choose to.

What beliefs are you clinging to, ask yourself? whether you're willing to attempt a new way of thinking, being, and acting and if they're helping you.

Add additional beliefs as time goes on by beginning one at a time.

If you want to find genuine love and happiness, start by taking that first step. Release what's limiting you and make a fresh decision.

Additional Tips For Finding Love

You should also take care of all the other necessary details when looking for true love, including:

- Join a reputable app or dating service right away if you aren't already.

- Update your profile if you're already a user of the applications. updating your "about me" section and adding fresh images.

- Step away from your comfort zone! Make it a point to follow your hobbies and passions to meet more men in real life.

- Attend dates that are ideal for developing genuine connections.

- On your dates, make sure you are talking about things that will deepen your connection and emotional closeness.

- Carry on! Every day, make one modest step on the correct path.

First-date conversation starters (Spark Chemistry Every time)

The Best Conversation Starters To Use

One of the secrets to a successful first date is to be prepared with a few smart questions that will spark a lively discussion and keep it going. The questions should ideally enable you to learn more about them and build an emotional bond that will make your time together enjoyable.

All the while letting you remain true to who you are. The date should, after all, be enjoyable for both of you.

1. To begin with, an open-ended topic makes for a terrific discussion opener. Avoid asking closed-ended questions that can be answered with a straightforward yes or no.

To avoid awkward pauses or lulls, open-ended questions give the dialogue a direction. In contrast, when the response is a straightforward yes or no, your conversation is at a standstill. So you're left attempting to keep the discussion lively and entertaining all the time.

2. Choose questions that are somewhat different from the standard, mundane ones you see every day.

You know the sort that most daters normally encounter. such as "What do you do for a living?" and "Do you have any siblings?" the sort that almost everyone asks but that adds nothing to the conversation.

First-date conversation starters (Guide On What To Say)

On a first date, use one of these fantastic conversation starters to keep the discussion going. Who knows, maybe not too long after that you'll go on your second date.

1. What sort of person are you seeking, first?

This is one of those off-the-cuff inquiries that will offer you some understanding of their beliefs, way of life, and areas of passion (like family, community, adventure, etc). Likewise, ask them about their dating goals.

You have the opportunity to be open and honest about the person you are searching for.

2. What do you do on the weekends?

Do they go to the gym, go on impromptu road trips, see a local band, or give their time to an animal shelter? Regardless of the response, asking someone how they spend their weekend may reveal a lot about their habits and interests.

in addition to their preferences, levels of physical activity, etc. encompassing the many kinds of connections that are also a part of their lives.

3. Tell me a fact about yourself that might surprise me.
This is a light-hearted first-date query that allows your date the chance to disclose a fact about themselves that they might not have otherwise considered. Possibly, they were too shy to bring up the subject on a first date. A great way to get to know each other's sense of humor is to share a humorous anecdote during this time.

4. Other than your parents, who has influenced you the most?

You may learn more about someone's values, their closest friends, and their interpersonal relationships by using this first-date discussion starter. Also considered are the dynamics of relationships and their capacity to last throughout time.

Further understanding of their long-term objectives for the future will be provided by this life question. Regarding their plans for a family and their intended job path

5. What are you most eagerly anticipating shortly?

You may learn more about someone's interests, aspirations for their profession, and way of life by asking them this. It's a good way to bond over something exciting they have coming up and to share something fantastic you have coming up.

6. What is the most impulsive action you have ever taken?

If you want to assess someone's sense of adventure and level of risk-taking, this is one of the finest things to ask on a first date. Additionally, it enables you to comprehend their level of flexibility.

7. Describe a normal day in your life.

Yes, this is similar to the weekend inquiry, but it allows for more open discussion about the respondent's daily activities, interests, and routines.

For instance, you could learn that they go to a personal trainer before or after work or that they meditate every morning. They could attend a reading club or play a certain sport in the evenings.

They are allowed to provide much more in response to this question than simply a brief response. over the traditional opening questions on a first date, such as "what do you do for a living?" or "how do you spend your free time?"

8. Did you make all of your travel arrangements in advance or did you just go with the flow on your most recent getaway? Another query that reveals information about someone's personality, way of life, and sense of adventure is this one.

Interesting side notes: According to a study by renowned psychologist Richard Wiseman (2), 18% of couples who discussed travel went on a second date. 9% of couples, on the other hand, tended to discuss movies extensively.

9. Do you now want a friend with whom you can share your life or just have fun?
On a first date, you may and should ask this question. It's obvious from the outset that this is a serious subject. This kind of unexpected inquiry might make some people uncomfortable, but never be hesitant to ask one. It's vital to find out as soon as you can if their aims are compatible with yours.

This will enable you to determine whether you envision a potential date with them sooner rather than later.

10. As a child, what did you wish to be?

On your first date, it's a great idea to connect and share your aspirations and dreams to keep the discussion flowing. It also provides you both an opportunity to talk about your upbringing. expanding the conversation beyond the traditional family-related inquiries that usually result in a (3) dull and lifeless debate.

11. Who do you know is the most fascinating?

It's frequently quite illuminating to discuss the other persons in their life who have inspired them, aside from parents and friends.

Peeling back the layers of their life depends on who they describe, such as a mentor, supervisor, spiritual leader, or coach. displaying a trait about themselves that isn't often discussed on a first date.

12. What kind of exercise do you prefer to do?

There is nothing wrong with having a few guilty pleasures, though. Most of the clients I work with want someone who leads an active, healthy lifestyle. if you think this is vital as well. You can determine if you are compatible in this area by asking questions on subjects like fitness and health.

And if you are? It also provides you with the ideal chance to arrange a second date to perform an activity you both like.

13. What was your most fascinating job to date?

One of the biggest attraction killers on a date has to be asking the person, "What do you do for a living?" Because it has a way of transforming a joyful and connecting first date into a humdrum feeling or job interview atmosphere.

Even while it's crucial to learn about your date's profession, work will inevitably come up. So why not stand out from the crowd? by providing them an opportunity to tell you a fascinating tale from their history.

14. What do you like best about your neighborhood?

You may talk about a wide range of topics when you ask someone how they feel about their home. Additionally, it expands the topic of conversation to popular locations in the neighborhood and discloses people's preferences for particular meals, hangouts, and retail establishments, among other things.

15. What was the most recent event you attended?

Did they attend a comedy show, play, athletic event, the symphony, a local band or music festival, or Shakespeare in the Park? Whatever comes up will offer you enough to speak about. Additionally, it provides a chance for friendships to develop around similar interests and values.

16. What do you appreciate most in a friendship?

If you want to know if this individual shares your beliefs and long-term objectives, bring up subjects related to personal connections. An excellent response to the "best friend" question.

17. Would you prefer?

When everything else fails, you should occasionally simply inject some humor into the situation. If the conversation is waning, playing a game of 20 questions, or would you rather can inject some much-needed flirting and fun into your evening? The inquiries may be provoking, illuminating, humorous, flirtatious, foolish, hot, or a combination of all of these!

18. Why?
Think Who, What, Where, When, Why, or How if all else fails.

It's sometimes not necessary to ask them another direct question if there are a lot of lulls or if one of you—or both of you—are feeling anxious. It's frequently preferable to elaborate on what they've previously said.

Asking them what it is about x that they love might help you connect with the emotional reason behind their response. What motivated you to perform X?

The debate continues once you address the emotional motive behind a person's actions. In addition to fostering a deeper connection than would be achieved by just moving on to the next inquiry.

What Characterizes a Good Conversation Starter?

For a first date, open-ended inquiries that encourage relaxation and a good time for both of you work best as conversation starters. opening up the conversation with questions. To find out if you two are compatible in terms of objectives, beliefs, and lifestyle beyond just physical appeal, get to know your date. In addition, establish an emotional connection right away to aid in deciding whether or not you two will go on more dates.

What Makes It Difficult To Find First Date Conversation Topics?

Theoretically, it shouldn't be difficult to come up with topics or things to say on a first date. What happens, though, if your worries get the better of you and you start to feel shy? Have you developed the syndrome of "I don't know what to say"? Or does it suddenly begin to resemble a job interview?

On a first date, there is often added pressure to impress and this might make you feel anxious. And can cause anyone to stumble or go completely blank when asked out on a date. Even those who regard themselves to be generally extraverted or adept at striking up conversations with strangers might experience it.

In light of this, it's a good idea to keep a couple of the greatest conversation starters and first-date questions on hand at all times. In case you stutter or the discussion ebbs, you know.

What to Say on a First Date to Continue the Conversation

Asking open-ended questions on a first date that strike a mix between personal, broad (such interests and activities), lighthearted, and in-depth is the greatest approach to keep the discussion going. In doing so, you'll provide the person you're speaking to the opportunity to say something intriguing about the subject at hand or about themselves, and the conversation will continue to flow smoothly.

Focusing on subjects that will help you learn more about each other's life on many levels is a wonderful idea as well. Which will enable the two of you to decide whether to go on a second or third date.

And keep it in mind when deciding what to talk about on a first date. The importance of listening is equal to that of talking.

Although they don't have to be, first dates may be awkward. Despite being shy, introverted, divorced, or long-term single. Or perhaps you simply want to experiment and liven up the discourse.

These first-date discussion themes may be a huge help in coming up with conversation starters, and they can also help you and your date have fun and feel excited about the outing.

Have A Wonderful Time Dating!